Frederick Douglass

Abolitionist and Author

Colonial Leaders

Lord Baltimore
English Politician and Colonist

Benjamin Banneker
American Mathematician and Astronomer

Sir William Berkeley
Governor of Virginia

William Bradford
Governor of Plymouth Colony

Jonathan Edwards
Colonial Religious Leader

Benjamin Franklin
American Statesman, Scientist, and Writer

Anne Hutchinson
Religious Leader

Cotton Mather
Author, Clergyman, and Scholar

Increase Mather
Clergyman and Scholar

James Oglethorpe
Humanitarian and Soldier

William Penn
Founder of Democracy

Sir Walter Raleigh
English Explorer and Author

Caesar Rodney
American Patriot

John Smith
English Explorer and Colonist

Miles Standish
Plymouth Colony Leader

Peter Stuyvesant
Dutch Military Leader

George Whitefield
Clergyman and Scholar

Roger Williams
Founder of Rhode Island

John Winthrop
Politician and Statesman

John Peter Zenger
Free Press Advocate

Revolutionary War Leaders

John Adams
Second U.S. President

Ethan Allen
Revolutionary Hero

Benedict Arnold
Traitor to the Cause

King George III
English Monarch

Nathanael Greene
Military Leader

Nathan Hale
Revolutionary Hero

Alexander Hamilton
First U.S. Secretary of the Treasury

John Hancock
President of the Continental Congress

Patrick Henry
American Statesman and Speaker

John Jay
First Chief Justice of the Supreme Court

Thomas Jefferson
Author of the Declaration of Independence

John Paul Jones
Father of the U.S. Navy

Lafayette
French Freedom Fighter

James Madison
Father of the Constitution

Francis Marion
The Swamp Fox

James Monroe
American Statesman

Thomas Paine
Political Writer

Paul Revere
American Patriot

Betsy Ross
American Patriot

George Washington
First U.S. President

Famous Figures of the Civil War Era

Jefferson Davis
Confederate President

Frederick Douglass
Abolitionist and Author

Ulysses S. Grant
Military Leader and President

Stonewall Jackson
Confederate General

Robert E. Lee
Confederate General

Abraham Lincoln
Civil War President

William Sherman
Union General

Harriet Beecher Stowe
Author of Uncle Tom's Cabin

Sojourner Truth
Abolitionist, Suffragist, and Preacher

Harriet Tubman
Leader of the Underground Railroad

Famous Figures of the Civil War Era

Frederick Douglass

Abolitionist and Author

Norma Jean Lutz

Arthur M. Schlesinger, jr.
Senior Consulting Editor

Chelsea House Publishers

Philadelphia

Produced by 21st Century Publishing and Communications, Inc.
New York, NY. http://www.21cpc.com

CHELSEA HOUSE PUBLISHERS
Production Manager Pamela Loos
Art Director Sara Davis
Director of Photography Judy L. Hasday
Managing Editor James D. Gallagher
Senior Production Editor J. Christopher Higgins

Staff for *FREDERICK DOUGLASS*
Project Editor Anne Hill
Associate Art Director Takeshi Takahashi
Series Design Keith Trego

The Chelsea House World Wide Web address is
http://www.chelseahouse.com

First Printing
1 3 5 7 9 8 6 4 2

Library of Congress Cataloging-in-Publication Data

Lutz, Norma Jean.
    Frederick Douglass / Norma Jean Lutz.
        p.   cm. — (Famous figures of the Civil War era)
    Includes bibliographical references and index.
    Summary: A biography of the man who, after escaping slavery,
became an orator, writer, and leader in the abolitionist movement in the
nineteenth century.
    ISBN 0-7910-6003-9 — ISBN 0-7910-6141-8 (pbk.)
        1. Douglass, Frederick, 1817?-1895—Juvenile literature. 2. Abolitionists—
United States—Biography—Juvenile literature. 3. Afro-American abolitionists—
Biography—Juvenile literature. 4. Antislavery movements—United States—
Juvenile literature. [1. Douglass, Frederick, 1817?-1895. 2. Abolitionists.
3. Afro-American—Biography.] I. Title. II. Famous figures of the Civil War era.

E449.D75 L88   2000
972.81'1—dc21   00-038394
[B]   CIP

Publisher's Note: In Colonial, Revolutionary War, and Civil War Era
America, there were no standard rules for spelling, punctuation,
capitalization, or grammar. Some of the quotations that appear in
the Colonial Leaders, Revolutionary War Leaders, and Famous
Figures of the Civil War Era series come from original documents
and letters written during this time in history. Original quotations
reflect writing inconsistencies of the period.

Contents

Frederick Douglass was born on a plantation where slaves worked in the fields, as shown here. His early life quickly taught him about the injustices of slavery.

Awakening to Slavery

Frederick Douglass was a slave child. He never knew the exact time, date, or place of his birth. In the early 1800s, the births of slave children were not recorded. He also never learned who his father was.

He did know that his mother was a slave. Her name was Harriet Bailey. She gave him an important-sounding name: Frederick Augustus Washington Bailey. The name Douglass was added much later in his life.

A name was about all Harriet could give to her son. She was not allowed to care for her little baby. She was owned by Captain Aaron Anthony. He lived in Talbot County on Maryland's Eastern Shore.

Slave women had to return to field work a week after their babies were born. When Harriet gave birth to Frederick in February 1817, she had no choice but to obey the rules of **slavery**.

There was a bright side to the situation. Harriet left Frederick in the loving care of an elderly couple, Grandmama Betsey and Grandpapa Isaac. This couple lived in a secluded cabin. It was 12 miles from the Great House of the **plantation**. Betsey and Isaac Bailey cared for many of the slave babies while the mothers worked. They also happened to be Frederick's grandparents.

Under the care of his devoted grandmama, Frederick knew nothing about the difficulties of slave life. He was safe and loved.

Grandmama Betsey had five daughters. They all worked long hours in the fields. In later years, Frederick remembered getting glimpses of his mother as she made hasty visits to him at night.

Frederick's grandparents, Betsey and Isaac, may have looked like this couple. They made sure Frederick felt loved and had enough to eat.

She had to walk for miles to reach the cabin. Then she hurried back to the other slaves. She had to be ready for the overseer's call to the fields. It came before the sun rose.

Frederick's grandmama was a talented woman. The other slaves respected her. Betsey knew how to make fishnets. She sold them in the nearby towns of Hillsboro and Denton. She used nets to catch fish for dinner.

Betsey also knew the secret of **preserving** seedling sweet potatoes through the winter. At planting time, she helped others plant the sweet potatoes. Many people believed that her "touch" brought good luck. The neighbors were careful to bring her part of the harvest. This extra food was a blessing because slaves were given very little to eat.

The Bailey cabin had a small loft with a ladder leading to it. There was also a fireplace. Not many slave cabins had a source of heat. Betsey buried her sweet potatoes in the dirt floor in front of this fireplace. It protected them from winter's frost.

Frederick's happy years in his grandmama's home came to an end all too quickly. He soon learned that Grandmama's house did not belong to her. Then he learned that his grandmother and all the children in her house belonged to someone Grandmama called "Old Master." The name was always spoken with fear and shuddering.

One hot day in August 1824, Grandmama Betsey took Frederick by the hand and told him to come along. Often he had walked with her to the town, but this time she did not go there. Instead they walked between great fields blanketed in heat. Soon they were both soaked in sweat.

Grandmama was quiet during the walk. Frederick knew something bad was about to happen. He clutched her skirts. After 12 long miles, they arrived at the Great House at Wye Place.

The Great House was both beautiful and frightening. Other slave children ran to greet them. Frederick learned that three of the children were his siblings. He hadn't known that he had any brothers and sisters. These children were strangers to him.

When he was seven, Frederick was taken to his owner's plantation house, like the one pictured here. Frederick was sad to leave his grandparents' loving care.

Frederick went into the back kitchen with his grandmother. They were given much-needed drinks of water. Betsey then urged Frederick to go outside and play with the others. Reluctantly, he obeyed, but he did not play. Rather, he stood back and watched from a distance.

Later, one of the children who had been with them in the kitchen came running out and said, "Fed, Fed, grandmama gone!"

Frederick was devastated. He rushed to the road, but she was not in sight. He threw himself on the ground and cried, beating the dust with his small fists. His older brother Perry tried to comfort him with a peach. Frederick threw it away.

The boy had never been deceived before. He cried himself to sleep that night. How could his dear grandmother who loved him so much leave him in this way? He did not know that his grandmother's heart was also breaking.

Frederick belonged to Captain Anthony. The captain worked for Colonel Edward Lloyd, who was a former governor of Maryland and a U.S. senator. He owned 20 or 30 large farms and nearly 1,000 slaves. These slaves were bought and sold whenever the owner wanted.

Captain Anthony had made his own fortune working for Colonel Lloyd. He bought his own farms and owned his own slaves. Both men had homes at Wye Place. Frederick lived in Captain Anthony's house. It stood in the shadow of Lloyd's Great House.

Slave children Frederick's age were kept by a slave woman known as Aunt Katy. As the household cook, Aunt Katy ran the place with an iron hand. She had to take care of all the young children at the main plantation.

Aunt Katy took an instant dislike to Frederick. She always found fault with what he was doing. If he misbehaved, she kicked him or gave him a whipping. Aunt Katy was nothing like Grandmama Betsey.

Captain Anthony didn't take the time to give food to each of the children. Instead he gave it to Aunt Katy. She decided which child got how much food. This power was used against Frederick. Aunt Katy often punished him by giving him very little food to eat.

The children were fed corn meal mush. After it was cooked, it was poured into a trough. The trough was placed on the floor or out in the yard.

The children ate with oyster shells or pieces of shingle. They never had spoons.

Slave children up to age 10 were given two long shirts a year. If the shirts wore out or were torn, they went naked. With no trousers, coats, or shoes, it was very hard to keep warm during the winter months. Frederick sometimes slept inside a feed bag in a kitchen pantry to keep warm.

One day when she was angry, Aunt Katy forced Frederick to go the entire day without food. That evening Frederick's mother happened to come to Wye House to visit him. She had brought some food wrapped in a handkerchief. Harriet scolded Katy for mistreating her son, then she cradled Frederick until he cried himself to sleep.

When he awoke, his mother was gone. He would never see her again. She died soon after the visit. Aunt Katy's treatment of Frederick never changed. But Frederick knew now that his mother loved him and cared about him.

The port of Baltimore looked much like this at the time
Frederick arrived there to live with the Auld family.
Frederick enjoyed his time in the city.

Touches of Kindness

rederick's owner, Captain Anthony, had a daughter named Lucretia who was married to a man named Thomas Auld. Lucretia Auld liked Frederick. The two began an odd sort of game. He would sing outside Lucretia's window. Upon hearing him, she sent him on an errand in exchange for food. By these actions, she very well may have saved Frederick from starving.

In time, Frederick somehow befriended Edward Lloyd's son, Daniel. Aunt Katy ordered Frederick to stay away from the Lloyds' house. He often disobeyed.

Daniel Lloyd had a private tutor. He spoke very good English. Frederick soon learned to imitate Daniel's speech.

One day Lucretia Auld gave Frederick wonderful news. In just three days, he was to leave Wye Place. He was going to live in Baltimore with Hugh Auld and his family. Hugh Auld was Lucretia's brother-in-law. "They were the three happiest days I had ever known," Frederick would later write. The eight-year-old boy scrubbed himself in the creek and got his first pair of trousers.

Baltimore was a busy shipbuilding center. Frederick loved the city. Best of all, Sophia Auld, Hugh's wife, was as kind to him as if he were her own son. In his new home, he had more than enough to eat and a warm straw bed. He was given the responsibility of running errands and overseeing two-year-old Tommy.

Because Hugh Auld was busy with his work and business, he paid little attention to the household. He was unaware that Sophia treated

Frederick like her own child.

Sophia had seldom been around slaves. She knew little about how they were to act. When Frederick hung his head in shame, as he had been taught, she would say, "Look up, child; don't be afraid." She taught him table manners, which were much different from eating at a wooden trough with an oyster shell.

After three years of this tender love, a message came from the Eastern Shore stating that Aaron Anthony had died. Anthony's estate and property, which included slaves, would be divided between his two children, Lucretia Auld and Andrew Anthony. Frederick would have to return to the plantation.

When Frederick left Baltimore, he, Sophia, and Tommy cried. They did not know if they would ever see each other again. Frederick was afraid of being given to Andrew Anthony. The man was cruel to his slaves.

At the plantation, the slaves were lined up along with the cattle, pigs, and horses to be divided or sold. "We had no more voice in the decision . . . than the oxen and cows that stood chewing at the haymow," Frederick wrote in later years.

Fortunately, Frederick was awarded to Lucretia Auld. She at once returned him to Baltimore. His joy knew no bounds! The Auld family and Frederick were so happy to be together again. Life in Baltimore quickly returned to normal.

Every day, Sophia read aloud to the boys from the Bible. This made Frederick curious. He knew there was some connection between the black marks on the page and the words Sophia spoke. He wanted to know how this worked. He asked Sophia if she would teach him to read. Sophia was pleased with his interest, so she agreed. Lessons began in earnest.

Sophia Auld was clearly unaware of the rules of slavery. She was very proud of Frederick's progress. One day she had Frederick read before her husband.

Thomas Auld was furious. He explained that

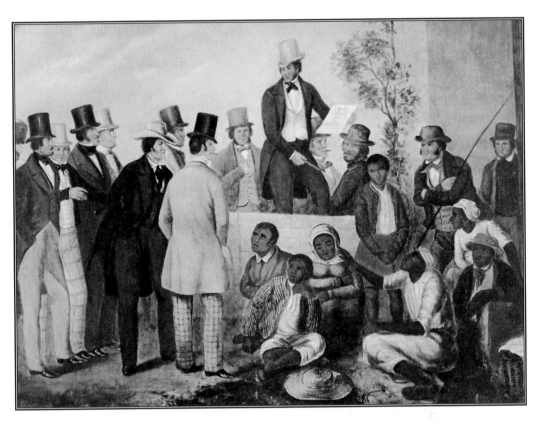

Slaves were bought and sold at slave markets like this one. In Baltimore, Frederick was amazed to find that some white people thought slavery was wrong.

it was against the law to teach a slave to read and write. He added that "if he learns to read the Bible it will forever unfit him to be a slave." Frederick heard these words. Suddenly he realized that learning to read could be his ticket to freedom.

Things changed from that moment. After facing her husband's anger, Sophia treated Frederick with less warmth. But although the Aulds forbade Frederick to ever read again, he secretly disobeyed them. He found old newspapers in the trash. He then sneaked them into his upstairs room and read them. He kept an old copy of Webster's spelling book. He asked his playmates to say words to him from the book.

Many of boys he played with were white boys. Frederick became close friends with them. He could openly talk to them about the terrible system of slavery. They listened with sympathy and understanding. In later years, Frederick commented that he never met a boy who defended the system of slavery. Their encouragement gave Frederick hope that one day he might be free.

From early on, Frederick had been taught that it was God's will for some people to be slaves and others to be owners. He knew slaves who believed that God required them to submit to slavery. Although this did not seem right, how could he argue? He did not have any information that went against what these people said.

From time to time, he had heard the word "abolition." He had no idea what it meant. And who could he ask? When he looked it up in the dictionary, he learn only that it meant "the act of abolishing."

At last, he read in a city newspaper that people had petitioned Congress. They were praying for the abolition of slavery. That was enough for Frederick. Now he knew there were white people who felt slavery was wrong. This was amazing news to a young slave boy.

When Frederick turned 13, he earned a bit of money blacking boots. With the money, he purchased a copy of the *Columbian Orator.* He'd heard his friends speak of it as something they used for school assignments.

The paper was filled with speeches against oppression and injustice. It supported human rights. Now, at last, he knew for sure. Slavery was neither God's idea nor God's plan. Slavery was wrong!

When he had time, Frederick practiced reading these speeches out loud. He felt it wasn't enough to have good ideas. It was important to be able to make the ideas clear to people who would listen.

The relationship between Frederick and Sophia continued to change. So did his friendship with young Tommy. When Frederick was a small boy, they could all be warm friends. But now that he was approaching manhood, his "family" began to treat him as the slave that he was. Sophia, he later commented, was unfit as a slave owner. "Nature made us friends, but slavery had made us enemies."

Losing Sophia's gentle treatment must have been painful for Frederick. But Sophia's prayers and Bible reading had had its effect on him. Later Frederick met a black man named Charles Lawson. He asked the older man about God.

Lawson told him to pray and to give his

problems to the Lord. Frederick did just that. This experience gave him inner peace. Lawson befriended the lonely boy and insisted that one day he would be a useful man in the world.

Frederick now knew two important things: slavery was wrong, and God would listen to his prayers. So Frederick began to pray for his own freedom.

One day at the wharf, Frederick saw two Irishmen unloading a boat. Without being asked, he stepped aboard and helped. When the work was done, the men started talking with Frederick. They asked him if he were a slave.

Frederick admitted that he was a "slave for life." The men sympathized with Frederick. They told him that he should run away. There would be friends in the North who would help him.

Frederick pretended that he wasn't interested in running away. But he learned something from the two men. He would need to learn to write as well as read. Then he could make forged passes. Without a pass, he could never hope to escape.

When Frederick learned to write, he used a quill pen like this one. He knew reading and writing would be important when he became a free man.

Frederick quickly began learning to write. He asked the boys in the neighborhood to help him. Instead of using paper and pen, he wrote with sticks in the dirt and with chalk on the pavement. He hid a barrel and a chair in his loft room. With the barrel as his desk, he taught himself to write by copying from the Bible and a hymnbook.

In 1833, Frederick's life again took a surprising turn. Soon he was wishing he had run away when the Irishmen suggested it. Thomas Auld and his brother Hugh Auld had an argument. Thomas demanded that Frederick be returned to the Eastern Shore. Going back had been difficult when Frederick was only 9. But now, 16-year-old Frederick was tall and muscular. He was very independent and smart. The idea of returning to the plantation was more difficult than ever.

Slaves often lived in large groups in poorly maintained houses and didn't have proper clothes or enough to eat. When Frederick went back to the plantation, he had to steal food to stay alive.

3

Moving Toward Freedom

Frederick soon learned that his friend Miss Lucretia had died in 1831. Her husband, Thomas Auld, now owned Frederick.

Mr. Auld had married again. His new wife, Rowena Auld, was the daughter of a wealthy slave owner. She was known for being very cruel to her slaves. She told her husband that he should work the slaves harder and feed them less.

For the first time since his days with Aunt Katy, Frederick knew what it was to be hungry. The only way he could get food was to steal it. But Frederick thought stealing was wrong. He didn't know what to do.

At last he decided that his master owned the food when it was being stored. If Frederick ate the food, it was still being kept in something the master owned. "He owned it in me," was how Frederick explained it.

Thomas and Rowena kept treating their slaves badly. Then a week-long church camp meeting was held in the area. Frederick saw his master go forward during the altar call. Frederick hoped Master Thomas would be different.

Nothing changed. In fact, things got worse.

Because he could read, Frederick was invited by other blacks to teach Sunday school at the home of a free black man. He gathered up a few old spelling books and New Testaments. The school began with 20 pupils.

At the second meeting, a mob of white men rushed in to break it up. The mob was led by Thomas Auld. Frederick's master decided that his slave was ruined. He thought Frederick was too smart for his own good. Auld decided to send Frederick to a man named Edward Covey.

Covey was known for being able to "break" any slave.

Covey was particularly hard on Frederick. For months the young black man was starved and worked almost to death. If he stopped to wipe the sweat from his face, he was beaten. The beatings tore his back into a mass of open flesh. Covey often hid from view. He'd leap out at the workers when they least expected it. The slaves nicknamed him "the snake."

On Sunday, the field slaves didn't work. All Frederick could do was collapse beneath a tree and nurse his wounds. He watched the sails of the ships out on the bay. Then he remembered that he could pray. He cried out to God to help him escape this bad situation.

One hot August day, Frederick collapsed from a heat stroke. Covey accused him of pretending to be sick. The man began to beat and kick Frederick. Unable to get up, he lay there helpless. Finally Covey left him alone.

Frederick couldn't believe that his master

meant for him to be treated this way. He waited for some strength to come back. Still bleeding, he then ran away to Thomas Auld.

Auld allowed him to stay the night. But the next morning, he told Frederick to go back to Covey. Full of fear, Frederick set out on the road, "feeling that I had no friend on earth, and doubting if I had one in heaven."

Covey was lying in wait for him. Driven by fear, Frederick ran and headed for the woods. Another slave named Sandy Jenkins helped Frederick. Sandy's wife was a free black. Sandy took him to a cabin that belonged to his wife. They fed Frederick and treated his wounds.

Frederick returned to Covey's farm when he got better. It was Sunday. Covey was in his wagon on the way to church. He sounded almost pleasant when he greeted Frederick.

On Monday morning, everything changed. Covey attacked, but Frederick was ready. He had decided that he would rather die than be beaten one more time.

Frederick endured beatings from Mr. Covey, a slave breaker like the man pictured here. However, no one could break Frederick's independent spirit.

Frederick did not hit the man. But he did resist. They wrestled for more than two hours. At last, Covey threw Frederick to the ground. "Now, you scoundrel, go to your work," he said. "I would not have whipped you half so hard if you had not resisted." The truth was, Frederick had not been whipped at all. Covey did not lay a hand on him again. Frederick finished out the year at the Covey farm. On December 25, 1834, he was sent back to Auld.

Frederick said that the moment when he stood up to Covey was a turning point in his life. Because he had not been afraid to die, he experienced the spirit of being free. "I was a *man* now, with renewed determination to be a *free man.*"

In January, Frederick was hired out to William Freeland. This man only cared that the work got done. At the Freeland farm, Frederick was once again working with Sandy Jenkins and several other young men. They became fast friends.

When they asked Freeland for permission to begin a Sunday school, the man agreed. He said that they could only discuss the Bible. But the young men were planning an escape. Sandy didn't want to go along with the plan. He had a bad dream that made him afraid of trying to escape.

Many slaves were allowed to travel on holidays. So the friends decided on the Easter holiday as their escape date. Frederick forged passes for each of them. Before they could act, someone told on them. They were caught and put in jail.

Frederick had been able to throw his pass into the fireplace before he was taken. The other men ate their passes. There was no proof that they had planned to escape.

The owners left Frederick and his friends in jail long enough to scare them. Thomas Auld visited Frederick in jail. He told the young slave that he would be sold to a man in Alabama.

Being sold into the "Deep South" was a frightening thing to a slave. Few slaves could survive the cruel treatment in those states.

Frederick did what his friends had done. He begged for forgiveness. He tried to look sorrowful. It's doubtful that his owner fell for the act. But Auld did change his mind. He decided to send Frederick back to Baltimore to learn a trade. Slaves who knew a trade were worth more money to an owner. Auld also told Frederick that he would free him when Frederick reached age 25. Frederick didn't really believe that promise, but he was happy for any reason to return to Baltimore.

Back at the Auld home in Baltimore, Frederick was treated more like a slave. Tommy never spoke to him except to ask him to do something.

Frederick's first job was in Gardiner's shipyards. Instead of learning a trade, he ran errands. At one time, both black and white men had worked side by side on the Baltimore docks. That had changed. White carpenters said they would no longer work with the blacks. They stated that unless the company owner let all the blacks go, they would refuse to work.

This situation opened Frederick's eyes. He began to understand some of the problems slavery brought to white people. The white workers at the shipyard were competing for jobs with black slaves who didn't get paid anything. More of the jobs went to the slaves.

Frederick saw how the unfairness of slavery harmed both black and white people. He felt it also made "slaves" of poor whites.

The workers on the docks began to threaten Frederick. One day he was attacked by four white men at once. More than 50 people stood by and watched. He was able to escape and make it home.

Sophia Auld nursed his wounds just as she would have done when he was a child. Her kindness almost made him think the beating was worth it.

Hugh Auld was angry that his man was beaten. He took the matter to court. He soon learned the problems black people faced. The word of a black man was not accepted in court. A white man could not testify on behalf of a black man.

Frederick said later, "If I had been killed in the presence of a thousand blacks, their testimony combined would have been insufficient to condemn a single murderer." To his credit, Hugh Auld was disgusted about these problems with the courts.

Auld did not send Frederick back to Gardiner's shipyard. Instead he took the young man with him to the shipyard where he also worked. Walter Price owned this business. Frederick learned to be an expert **caulker**.

His wages were placed directly into the hands of Hugh Auld at the end of every week. It made Frederick angry. "I . . . earned it, . . . it was paid to me, and it was *rightfully* my own; and yet, upon every returning Saturday night, this money–my own hard earnings, every cent of it–was demanded of me, and taken from me by Master Hugh."

That wasn't all that upset Frederick. Hugh Auld would carefully count the money. Then he'd look up at Frederick and ask, "Is that all?"

On the brighter side, Mr. Auld allowed Frederick more freedom in his spare time. The young man was well over six feet tall. In spite of years of harsh treatment, he was very handsome. Other young black people liked him.

Frederick began to attend meetings with free young blacks. Through this group, Frederick became active in the **Underground Railroad**. He helped escaped slaves make their way to freedom.

He learned how slaves escaped. He got to know what contacts they could make along the way.

A young lady named Anna Murray also attended the meetings. Frederick liked Anna very much. But he was a slave. What could a slave offer a free girl? He promised her that if he ever gained his freedom, he would send for her.

Frederick learned more and more about freedom. He knew he must escape to the North. He had not forgotten his days in jail. Escape could be very dangerous. If he were caught, he could be returned to Thomas Auld. Then he would be sold down the river into the Deep South. But once he made the decision, there was no turning back.

It took about three weeks to complete his plan. He borrowed a sailor uniform from a friend. He took the sailor's protection papers with him. If anyone looked closely, they would quickly realize that the papers described a man who looked nothing like Frederick. He just hoped no one would pay too much attention to him.

On the day of his escape, Frederick arrived at

Frederick escaped from Maryland on a train like this one. After two train rides and time on a ship, Frederick was a free man in New York.

the train station just in time to jump on the train. He grabbed his luggage that his friends had placed there earlier. Then the conductor sold Frederick a ticket. Would the man notice anything wrong?

The man barely glanced at the papers. Frederick's sailor uniform helped. And Frederick had been around ships and sailors long enough to pick up the talk. "I could talk sailor like an 'old salt,'" he later recalled.

The fear he felt as the train sped along made his heart pound. Time dragged by slowly. "Minutes were hours," he wrote in his biography, "and hours were days." He was as scared as "a murderer fleeing from justice."

The train carried him through Maryland into Delaware. At Wilmington, Delaware, he boarded a ship. This ship sailed to Philadelphia. From there he took another train to New York. At long last, he was standing on free soil. He could hardly believe it. He walked from the ferry to Broadway. New York's busy crowds hurried all around him.

The "dreams of my childhood and the purposes of my manhood were now fulfilled," Frederick later wrote. "A free state around me, and a free earth under my feet. What a moment was this to me."

Frederick didn't know anyone in New York. He had no money. For the moment, that did not matter. He was a free man at last!

Industry in the North was very different from what Frederick had seen in the South. He was surprised to see how well businesses did without slaves.

Speaking Out for Freedom

Back in Baltimore, Anna received the message she had been waiting for: Frederick was free. She lost no time in getting to New York. The two were married right away.

Frederick had found shelter in the home of David Ruggles. Mr. Ruggles worked in the Underground Railroad. Frederick and Anna's wedding took place in Ruggles's home. The minister was also a runaway slave.

From David Ruggles, Frederick learned that New Bedford, Massachusetts, was a great shipping center. Caulkers were needed. With his new bride by his side,

Frederick took the stagecoach to New Bedford. There the couple contacted Nathan Johnson. He was another worker in the Underground Railroad.

Mr. Johnson urged Frederick to change his name. Then it would be harder for people to find him and take him back to the South.

Mr. Johnson had been reading the book *Lady of the Lake* by Sir Walter Scott. He suggested Frederick use the name Douglas. It was the name of one of the people in the book. Frederick agreed, but he added another *s*. From then on, he called himself Frederick Douglass.

The town of New Bedford was very different to Frederick. He was surprised at how well-off people were without slaves. In the South, any white person who didn't have slaves was very poor. He had been told that it was that way everywhere.

In New Bedford, he saw that people who worked hard earned good pay. They bought homes, land, and other things. They thought well of themselves.

Free blacks were also proud and worked hard. Frederick had always been told that blacks were lazy and good-for-nothing. Now he knew this wasn't true.

He was amazed to learn that an ox that cost only $60 did the same work as dozens of slaves. The slaves cost about $1,000 each. This meant that the ox did much more work for much less money. People in the North also invented all kinds of labor-saving devices.

Frederick noticed that something was missing. There were "no loud songs heard from those engaged in loading and unloading ships." He knew that slaves who worked in the fields often sang out in order to express their feelings and endure the hardship.

These new scenes helped Frederick see things more clearly. Slave owners kept their slaves from finding out the truth. Because the slaves couldn't read, they only knew what their masters told them. Frederick believed that education was one of the main keys to true freedom.

Frederick and Anna had a hard time that first winter. Even in New England, people were **prejudiced**. The shipping companies would not hire a black man as a caulker until all the white men had jobs.

Frederick didn't mind this problem. He was young and strong and very happy to be free. He found odd jobs. Working long hours didn't bother him. Now all the money he earned was his to keep.

The Douglasses became members at New Bedford's Zion Chapel. They met in a small schoolhouse on Second Street. Church became a safe place for Frederick and Anna. The pastor there was a runaway slave named Thomas James.

Pastor James spoke out against slavery whenever he had the chance. Thomas James gave Frederick his first opportunities to speak in public.

Frederick was happy to be free. But he also was confused. Part of him wanted to forget about slavery forever. The other part wanted to work against slavery. Should he speak out too?

Frederick began attending every **antislavery** meeting held in his town. He wanted to learn more.

A few months after arriving in New Bedford, Frederick was given a copy of the *Liberator*. This was an antislavery newspaper put out by William Lloyd Garrison. Garrison was a small man who wore glasses. He was fast becoming the loudest voice in America against slavery. He also spoke out for women's rights.

By reading the paper, Frederick became familiar with Mr. Garrison's ideas. Soon William Garrison was Frederick's hero. Then the man came to New Bedford to speak. Frederick was right there to hear him.

At that meeting, Frederick heard Garrison say, "Prejudice against color [is] rebellion against God." How good it was to hear a white person say the things he'd always believed in his heart.

By now Frederick and Anna were parents of two children. Rosetta was born June 24, 1839. Lewis Henry came the next year on October 2.

Frederick was proud of his children. He loved them dearly.

Antislavery groups in New Bedford asked Frederick to speak to them. In 1841, he was surprised to be asked to speak at an antislavery convention in Nantucket, Massachusetts. The bigger surprise was that he would share the stage with William Lloyd Garrison.

When Frederick gave his speech, he trembled. But afterwards, he was invited to become a traveling speaker for the Massachusetts Anti-Slavery Society.

Frederick was very busy during the next few years. He traveled and spoke in many places. Sometimes the crowds didn't care. Other times they were friendly.

Maria Chapman was one of the founders of the Boston Female Antislavery Society. She edited the *Liberator* when William Lloyd Garrison was away on lecture tours.

In 1835, a mob surrounded one of the society's meetings. Mrs. Chapman knew that black members were in special danger. The mob might try to kill them. She told each white member to hook arms with a black member. Then two-by-two, the women marched from the hall.

The crowd roared in anger. The women kept on marching. They arrived at Mrs. Chapman's home safely. There, the meeting continued.

William Lloyd Garrison was Frederick's hero. Garrison spoke out not only against slavery, but also for women's rights.

Many times the people were very angry.

One time in Ohio, Frederick and his friends weren't allowed to speak in a building. They built a stage at the edge of town. A crowd gathered to listen. Then a mob of people began throwing rocks and rotten eggs.

The people on the stage pretended nothing was happening. It didn't work. Finally a fight broke out. During the ruckus, Frederick's hand was broken.

Such scenes never stopped Frederick. He cared too much about ending slavery. Many people had never understood how unfair slavery was. Then they heard Frederick, an escaped slave, tell stories about his life. The people began to change their minds.

Frederick faced many dangers when he spoke. If his real name were discovered, he could be returned to his master.

Because Frederick spoke so well, some people refused to believe that he'd ever been a slave. They expected a slave to hang his head and use "plantation talk." Frederick decided to write a book about his life. He felt it would silence these doubts forever.

In 1845, Frederick wrote and published *Narrative of the Life of Frederick Douglass.* He gave actual names, specific dates, and real locations to prove that he truly had been a slave. Shortly after the book's release, he learned that the Aulds had been told about it. They decided that they wanted to reclaim their "property."

Frederick's new friends encouraged him to leave the country. He and Anna now had two more children, Frederick Junior, and Charles. While Frederick hated to leave Anna with the four children, he had no choice but to go. Shortly thereafter, he and his friend James Buffum left for Europe.

In 1850, Congress passed the Fugitive Slave Law. It stated that anyone who helped an escaping slave was breaking the law. That person could be fined or sent to prison.

The law also gave certain people the right to arrest and return runaway slaves. These people could reward other people for catching runaways.

Professional slave hunters didn't just find slaves. They also captured free blacks and made slaves of them. People who had once felt safe in New York, Philadelphia, and Boston fled to Canada. There, they were truly safe.

When Frederick went to London, he saw many beautiful buildings, including St. Paul's Cathedral (shown here). In Europe, he was happy to see black and white people treated equally.

Sounds
of War

Frederick's time abroad changed his life. He noticed a difference from the moment he arrived in England. Everyone treated him as an equal.

He spent months giving speeches in many of the major cities in Europe. These speeches raised money for the antislavery cause in America.

In Great Britain, slavery had ended in 1833. Organized antislavery groups still met. They worked to get America to end slavery as well. Frederick, the escaped slave, was brought into some of the finest homes in Great Britain where he made lifelong friends.

He showed a sense of humor as he wrote about

these meetings. "When the door was opened, I walked in on a footing with my white fellow citizens, and, from all I could see, I had as much attention paid me by the servants . . . as any with a paler skin. As I walked through the building the statuary did not fall down, the pictures did not leap from their places, the doors did not refuse to open."

Then two British women did something that Frederick had never expected. It was a wonderful gift. They bought his freedom from Thomas Auld. When Frederick returned to the United States in 1847, he was truly a free man. He didn't have to be afraid of being made a slave again.

As soon as Frederick returned to America, he got to work. He used the money he had raised from his trip and bought a printing press. He put out his own newspaper. It was called the *North Star*. He chose that name because slaves escaped by following the north star at night.

Next Frederick moved his family to Rochester, New York. He kept working hard to end slavery.

The *North Star* became Frederick's voice to the country.

Frederick soon learned that he didn't agree with his hero, Mr. Garrison, about some things. William Garrison believed the best way to end slavery was to break up the United States. Then slave states would not be protected by the navy or army.

Frederick strongly disagreed. Breaking up the nation would leave slaves at the mercy of their owners. He thought that only violence would convince the South to release the slaves. Frederick let people know what he thought. Many people who followed Garrison went against Frederick.

As the nation moved into the 1850s, major conflicts spread across the land. Everyone disagreed over slavery. People in the new territory of Kansas were deciding whether it would be a slave state or a free state. Pro-slavery and anti-slavery groups moved into the territory. They fought with each other. The state was nicknamed "Bloody Kansas."

One of the people who traveled to Kansas was John Brown. He fought along with his five sons. He believed that steps had to be taken to free all the slaves.

Brown came from North Elba, New York. He had previously worked with Frederick in the antislavery cause. John Brown changed Frederick's life more than any other person except William Garrison. But in 1857, Brown and Frederick disagreed about what should be done.

At about the same time, the Supreme Court made a ruling that was called the Dred Scott decision. The high court stated that black people were not citizens. They could not take a case

Anthony Burns was a slave who had escaped from his owner in Virginia. He lived a peaceful life in Boston until he was arrested in 1851.

Abolitionists held a mass meeting to protest his arrest. The angry crowd stormed the courthouse to set Burns free. Army troops were called in to get Burns first. With flags flying at half-mast and bells tolling, Burns was marched to the harbor. There, he was put aboard a ship headed for Virginia.

Northerners became very angry. Nine states passed personal-liberty laws designed to protect blacks in their areas.

to court. The ruling stated that blacks "have no rights which the white man is bound to respect."

Some people thought the Dred Scott decision would settle the fight over slavery. Instead many people became very angry. Terrible violence broke out.

Brown returned to New York. He talked to Frederick about a plan to help slaves. He wanted to attack the federal **arsenal** at Harper's Ferry, Virginia. An arsenal is a place where guns, bullets, and other weapons are stored.

When Frederick heard this idea, he strongly disagreed. He told his friend that such an attack would turn the entire country against them. Frederick begged Brown to change his mind. Brown urged Frederick to be a part of his plan.

Neither person would budge. When Brown left, Frederick was sad. He knew that he would never see his friend alive again.

He was right. The October 1859 attack on Harper's Ferry failed. Many of Brown's men were killed. Brown was captured, found guilty

John Brown and his followers needed a hideout before they attacked Harper's Ferry. They rented the Kennedy farm. It was about five miles north of the ferry. Dense trees surrounded it.

Brown feared that a home filled with men might make people suspicious. His daughter and daughter-in-law joined them. The long wait was hard. The men were cooped up indoors all day. They could only play checkers, read, and argue. The women acted as lookouts. When it was almost time for the attack, the two women were sent home to New York.

at trial, and sentenced to death by hanging. The sentence was carried out on December 2, 1859.

Brown had letters from Frederick. These letters were found after he was caught. Rumors spread that Frederick was going to be arrested. Frederick left the country and traveled to England.

His visit only lasted for a few months. Then he got very bad news. His youngest daughter, Annie, had died. Frederick loved his daughter very much. He called her the "light and life of my house." He rushed home to be with his family.

Frederick was very sad. But he still had much work to do. Abraham Lincoln was running for president. Frederick could see that Lincoln was by

A soldier takes John Brown to jail. Frederick was Brown's friend but disagreed with him over the use of violence in the fight against slavery.

far the best choice for the job. He did everything he could to help get Abraham Lincoln elected.

Lincoln was elected president. However, even

Abraham Lincoln raises the flag at Philadelphia's Independence Hall. Frederick had worked hard to get Lincoln elected.

before he took office, the Southern states had begun breaking away from the Union. Then in April 1861, Southern forces attacked and fired on Fort Sumter, South Carolina. The Civil War had begun.

Right away, Frederick asked the government to use black soldiers in the war. He reminded them that the South was using slaves to build forts and dig trenches. This left more white soldiers free to fight for the South. Why not let free black men fight for the North? He wrote letters about this idea to many leaders.

Frederick was very upset that the president did not free the slaves as soon as the war started. Finally on January 1, 1863, President Lincoln signed the **Emancipation** Proclamation. It freed all the slaves who had been held captive for so long.

Wild celebrations were held all across the nation. Frederick spoke at a gathering in Boston. In spite of his joy, he knew the work had only begun.

Finally, word came that units of black soldiers were going to be organized in Massachusetts. Frederick's sons, Charles and Lewis, were among the first to enlist.

Many white officers were unhappy with this

This recruitment poster for black soldiers featured the slogan, "Come Join Us Brothers." Frederick worked toward getting equal pay for blacks who joined the army.

decision. They did not want to lead black soldiers into battle. The soldiers fought anyway. They stood in the front lines of many battles. They won many honors for doing a good job.

Frederick kept asking Congress to give black soldiers equal pay and equal treatment. At last, he was asked to make a personal visit to the president. After his visit, Frederick found that he liked President Lincoln even more. "I at once felt myself in the presence of an honest man," he said, "one whom I could love, honor, and trust without reserve or doubt."

The end of the war in April 1865 brought great joy to citizens all across the nation. However, the joy soon turned to tremendous sadness. President Lincoln was shot and killed.

At a meeting in Rochester, Frederick spoke to a crowd. He talked about how much he had loved the great leader Abraham Lincoln.

Mrs. Lincoln later presented Frederick with one of her husband's walking sticks. He was very honored and proud to have it.

This painting shows Washington, D.C., at the time Frederick moved there. He was the first black man to become marshal of the District of Columbia.

6

The Work
Goes On

The slaves were free, but Frederick's work was far from over. He knew the former slaves needed a helping hand. Most of them could not read or write. They had very few clothes and no money. They didn't own homes or land. Where would they live? How could they get jobs?

Frederick kept speaking out. He wanted equal rights for all black people. He asked Congress to set up a way to help freed slaves. They needed medical treatment. They needed schooling and financial help.

Congress agreed. It set up the Freedmen's Bureau. Frederick was asked to take charge of it. He said no. He did not trust the new president, Andrew Johnson.

New laws helped the freed slaves of the South. The Civil Rights Act of 1866 gave all slaves citizenship. The Fourteenth Amendment gave all black men the right to vote.

By the 1870s, Frederick's friends and family convinced him to stop working so hard. He sold the *North Star* newspaper and moved from New York State to Washington, D.C. Their new home sat on nine acres. They called it Cedar Hill. It overlooked the Capitol.

Cedar Hill had barns and large vegetable and flower gardens. They reminded him of the gardens he and Anna had enjoyed in their old home. The next year, Frederick purchased 15 more acres. Cedar Hill was

It took two years for Congress to agree to start the Freedmen's Bureau. The bureau was designed to take care of anything to do with freed slaves. It depended on the War Department for money and staff.

The Bureau sold and rented lands that had been taken from their owners during the war. President Johnson returned all land to the pre-Civil War owners in 1866. After that, freed slaves couldn't use the land. Despite its problems, the bureau helped African Americans gain some of the rights that they were denied during slavery.

a grand place. It was very different from the dirt-floor cabin where he had played as a child.

Frederick still found work to do. He became head of the Freedmen's Savings and Trust Company. This bank was set up to help black people get business loans. When Frederick took over the bank, it had many problems. He couldn't fix them. The bank was forced to close.

In 1877, President Rutherford B. Hayes made Frederick the marshal of Washington, D.C. This was one of the highest offices ever given to a black man.

It seemed that making Frederick the marshal of Washington, D.C., was an important step in America. The job might help more white people accept blacks as equals. But President Hayes wasn't really working to make black people equal. Behind the scenes, he was cutting back on things that had been done for the blacks.

President Hayes also changed what the marshal did. The marshal used to stand beside the president during important visits. He would introduce guests to the president. Frederick never was asked to do this part of the job.

While he was marshal, Frederick decided to visit his old home on the Eastern Shore of Maryland. He wanted to see his old master, Thomas Auld. Frederick was shown to his old master's bedroom. Auld was dying. He was shaking from his illness. He wept when he saw his former slave. Frederick was so choked up he could barely speak.

They spoke of Grandmama Betsey Bailey, whom Frederick had loved so much. He finally learned the truth about her last days. She had been purchased by Auld's brother-in-law. Then she had been taken to the town of St. Michaels. She was cared for until her death. This news comforted Frederick.

On August 4, 1882, Anna died from a stroke. She was buried in Rochester, New York, where the Douglasses had lived for so many years. After his wife's death, Frederick was very sad. He had always worked hard. Now he couldn't even give speeches. Friends whisked him away to a quiet spot in Maine. He rested and got better.

Two years later, Frederick made big news. He married a white woman in Washington, D.C. Helen Pitts was 45 years old, 20 years younger than Frederick. The marriage caused quite a stir among both friends and family. In spite of the talk about his marriage, Frederick was still in demand as a speaker. He and Helen seemed to be very happy.

Frederick and Helen traveled abroad. They ended their trip in Africa. Frederick wanted to learn more about the "science of the races." He longed to end the claims that Africans were an inferior race. He tried to prove that the blacks of interior Africa were related to the people who founded the great kingdoms of Egypt.

In June 1889, President Benjamin Harrison appointed Frederick Douglass as a minister to the island of Haiti. Frederick said yes. But the hot weather bothered Frederick. He also had to deal with hard problems. After two years,

Frederick retired. He was the first black person to serve as a foreign minister.

Frederick and Helen returned to Cedar Hill. There he could enjoy his grandchildren and his great-grandchildren. It was one of the happiest times of his life. He didn't speak in public as often, but he was still busy. He organized his papers and writings. He updated his book by adding more than 100 pages. Its new title was *Life and Times of Frederick Douglass*. It was printed in the fall of 1892.

The lack of progress in the lives of blacks throughout the South bothered Frederick. Stories of **lynchings** upset him. Unlike the days before the Civil War, few people cared.

On February 20, 1895, Frederick rode into the city from Cedar Hill. He was going to attend a rally for women's rights. Back home after the meeting, he and Helen had an early supper. They planned on attending a local black church for an evening service.

As he was joking about one of the speakers

When Frederick died, speeches and music commemorated his life, which he had dedicated to helping people who faced injustice.

he'd heard that day, the giant of a man crumpled to the floor. The great abolitionist was dead.

On the day of his funeral, schools were closed.

Thousands of children filed past his casket in the African Methodist Episcopal Church in Washington, D.C., where a service was held. Then Frederick's children and his wife took his body on the train to Rochester, New York. There, another service was held. He was buried beside his first wife, Anna, and his beloved daughter Annie.

Some have said that Frederick was one of the greatest speakers of the 1800s. He changed countless lives throughout the course of his life. He wanted to be thought of as just a man, but people looked at him as unusual. He was an educated, runaway slave. In the end, he kept that image alive through his many writings and speeches. They described the trials of his slave days in ways that people will never forget.

Until the day he died, Frederick worked to increase his knowledge and to improve the lives of those who still suffered from prejudice.

GLOSSARY

abolitionist–a person who is in favor of getting rid of slavery

antislavery–that which is against slavery

arsenal–a place for storing or making arms and ammunition

caulker–a person who makes a wooden boat watertight by packing the seams

emancipation–the act of making free

fugitive–a person who flees; a runaway

liberator–a person who sets another person free

lynching–a mob action in which a person is put to death

plantation–a large estate or farm on which crops are grown and harvested by workers who live there

preserving–to keep free from decay

prejudice–an opinion of a person or group formed without looking at the facts fairly

slavery–the state in which one person is owned by another person

Underground Railroad–a network of places and people that helped slaves escape to freedom

CHRONOLOGY

1817   Born in February on a plantation in Maryland and named Frederick Augustus Washington Bailey.

1825   Becomes property of Hugh Auld in Baltimore.

1834   Delivered to slave breaker Edward Covey.

1838   Escapes to the North; changes his name to Frederick Douglass; marries Anna Murray.

1841   Speaks before a group of abolitionists in Nantucket, Massachusetts; sets out on a speaking tour.

1845   Publishes his autobiography, *Narrative of the Life of Frederick Douglass.*

1847   Founds an antislavery newspaper called the *North Star.*

1855   Publishes his second book, *My Bondage and My Freedom.*

1861–65   Helps recruit blacks for the Union Army.

1877   Is appointed the marshal of Washington, D.C., one of the highest offices ever given to a black man.

1882   Anna Douglass dies.

1884   Marries Helen Pitts.

1889–91   Serves as minister to Haiti.

1895   Dies on February 20; is buried in Rochester, New York.

CIVIL WAR TIME LINE

1860   Abraham Lincoln is elected president of the United States on November 6. During the next few months, Southern states begin to break away from the Union.

1861   On April 12, the Confederates attack Fort Sumter, South Carolina, and the Civil War begins. Union forces are defeated in Virginia at the First Battle of Bull Run (First Manassas) on July 21 and withdraw to Washington, D.C.

1862   Robert E. Lee is placed in command of the main Confederate army in Virginia in June. Lee defeats the Army of the Potomac at the Second Battle of Bull Run (Second Manassas) in Virginia on August 29–30. On September 17, Union general George B. McClellan turns back Lee's first invasion of the North at Antietam Creek near Sharpsburg, Maryland. It is the bloodiest day of the war.

1863   On January 1, President Lincoln issues the Emancipation Proclamation, freeing slaves in Southern states. Between May 1–6, Lee wins an important victory at Chancellorsville, but key Southern commander Thomas J. "Stonewall" Jackson dies from wounds. In June, Union forces hold the city of Vicksburg, Mississippi, under siege. The people of Vicksburg surrender on July 4. Lee's second invasion of the North during July 1–3 is decisively turned back at Gettysburg, Pennsylvania.

1864	General Grant is made supreme Union commander on March 9. Following a series of costly battles, on June 19 Grant successfully encircles Lee's troops in Petersburg, Virginia. A siege of the town lasts nearly a year. Union general William Sherman captures Atlanta on September 2 and begins the "March to the Sea," a campaign of destruction across Georgia and South Carolina. On November 8, Abraham Lincoln wins reelection as president.
1865	On April 2, Petersburg, Virginia, falls to the Union. Lee attempts to reach Confederate forces in North Carolina but is gradually surrounded by Union troops. Lee surrenders to Grant on April 9 at Appomattox, Virginia, ending the war. Abraham Lincoln is assassinated by John Wilkes Booth on April 14.

FURTHER READING

Douglass, Frederick. *Escape from Slavery: The Boyhood of Frederick Douglass in His Own Words.* Edited by Michael McCurdy. New York: Alfred A. Knopf, 1994.

McKissack, Frederick and Patricia. *Rebels Against Slavery: American Slave Revolts.* New York: Scholastic, 1996.

Meltzer, Milton. *They Came in Chains: The Story of Slave Ships.* New York: Benchmark Books, 2000.

Pryor, Bonnie. *Joseph: 1861 A Rumble of War.* New York: Morrow Junior Books, 1999.

Whitmore, Arvella. *Trapped Between the Lash and the Gun.* New York: Dial Books for Young Readers, 1999.

INDEX

PICTURE CREDITS

page

3: The Library of Congress
6: National Archives
9: National Archives
12: New Millennium Images
16: New Millennium Images
21: National Archives
26: New Millennium Images
28: The Library of Congress
33: The Library of Congress
40: New Millennium Images
42: The Library of Congress
49: National Archives
52: New Millennium Images
59: New Millennium Images
60: The Library of Congress
62: The Library of Congress
64: New Millennium Images
71: The Library of Congress

ABOUT THE AUTHOR

NORMA JEAN LUTZ, who lives in Tulsa, Oklahoma, has been writing professionally since 1977. She is the author of more than 250 short stories and articles as well as more than 40 books–fiction and nonfiction. Of all the writing she does, she most enjoys writing children's books.

Senior Consulting Editor **ARTHUR M. SCHLESINGER, JR.** is the leading American historian of our time. He won the Pulitzer Prize for his book *The Age of Jackson* (1945), and again for *A Thousand Days* (1965). This chronicle of the Kennedy Administration also won a National Book Award. He has written many other books, including a multi-volume series, *The Age of Roosevelt.* Professor Schlesinger is the Albert Schweitzer Professor of the Humanities at the City University of New York, and has been involved in several other Chelsea House projects, including the COLONIAL LEADERS series of biographies on the most prominent figures of early American history.